I0468187

Write a Step-by-Step Book: Write Fast, Write More, Solve Problems, Write Bestsellers

By Dean Giles

Legal Disclaimer

Introduction

Break it down! Simplify! Spell it out! Make it easy to follow. If a picture is worth a thousand words, a model is worth a thousand dollars. The world of nonfiction books is a world where people have difficult and vexing problems. They need real solutions to those problems, and they need someone that can show them how to solve those problems, step-by-step.

I've read hundreds of nonfiction books. I have searched out the books looking for answers. I have found some of those books to be very entertaining, I have found others to be very informative, but the ones that have made my life easier and have changed my way of thinking were the ones with straight forward and simple instructions. These are the ones that sit on my bookshelf and that I return to again and again. They make great reference volumes, because they are, by design, compact and to the point.

Where most nonfiction books come up short is that they don't have specific enough instructions. They are usually really good at pointing out what the problems are and what benefits you, the reader, will receive when you solve your particular problems. But they are light on the specific, easy-to-follow steps that will actually solve the problem!

I also realized that, with those books, where the authors do a good job of presenting the problems and promise solutions, as a reader, I often get to a point where I am salivating—I have experienced that problem, I REALLY want the solution! However, by the end of the book, I am usually disappointed. It is true, that most books offer a solution, but rarely do they provide detailed enough instructions to really help me put the solution to work for me.

YES I KNOW: to solve my weight problems I simply have to eat fewer calories and increase exercise, to solve my money problems I simply must bring in more money and spend less, to solve my relationship problem I need to be kinder and think of others more often, to solve my career problem I need to show leadership and innovation, somehow all of that is so painfully obvious, and yet so mystifyingly illusive.

The truth is, each of us knows more than we realize. Each of us, for the most part, has a basic understanding of how things work. Sometime we DO need a better solution, but often, what we really need is a better way to implement what we already know. We need something that will entice us to work our way over the barriers, and actually put into action what we have learned.

That is where the step-by-step book comes in to play. Writing a step-by-step book solves a number of problems. For one thing, it simplifies the process for the author. For another, it makes the solution seem easier and more doable for the reader. Step-by-step instructions seem more manageable. They can be accomplished one at a time. The reader can eat the proverbial elephant, one bite at a time, and avoid the inevitable "drinking from the fire hydrant" effect of the typical overload of information that comes from most informational books.

You Already Know Much of What You Will Need to Write – And It Is All Brilliant!

How many problems have you solved in your lifetime? Can you simplify the process of solving one specific problem to a set of steps that anyone could take to solve that problem? Can you add your own introduction to the problem by explaining what situations in your life led up to the crisis? Were there some solutions that you tried that didn't work? Did others give you advice that helped you along the way, or did the advice not really help at all? How did you feel when everyone "had advice for you to solve your problem"? And how did it feel when you realized that for all the good intentions, the advice was obvious? What do you wish you had known before you started on the road to your ultimate solution? What were the results of implementing the solution? Can you summarize the steps and the results in a closing conclusion?

If you can answer the questions above, you can write a step-by-step book that will actually help a lot of people solve their biggest problems. Your book could be what makes the difference for them. It could be the "manual" for a better life for them. If you suffered from a problem, then it stands to reason that lots of other people are also suffering from the same problem. If you have solved that problem, you have a valuable solution that needs to be shared with others, and that others will gladly pay for!

Perhaps you might think that it would be embarrassing to write about a problem that you have experienced. That is a perfectly reasonable thing to feel. In that case simply write the book in the third person. Explain that you helped a friend or an associate to solve this problem in their lives. Perhaps you could write your book as an accumulation of experiences from more than one person experiencing this problem. You can also write your book with a pen name, no one else has to know that you are the author! There are so many options here.

You actually may be the go-to person that others come to when they experience these kinds of problems. In that way, you become the local expert. You have information that others need. You can help others, and help yourself, by getting the solutions to these problems into an easy to follow step-by-step book.

And, what if you don't have all of the answers? That's OK too. I am going to show you the best places to quickly find the answers to those difficult problems, keeping in mind that the solutions are rarely new or earth-shaking. The best solutions are the simple, straight forward solutions! The magic comes in the presentation of the solution and how exactly to implement the solution. The magic really is in the step-by-step presentation that will motivate your reader to take those steps and make a change in his or her life. You can be that catalyst and be the influencer that gets people to a better place through your book.

I am going to make one more bold statement. You actually need to publish your book as an eBook. Ebooks and Information Products are creating a new economy. Amazon announced that they are selling more eBooks than physical books. People like John Locke and Amanda Hocking have self-published and sold millions of eBooks. Market places for eBooks can be found all over, from Clickbank, to Amazon, from JVZoo to Barnes and Noble, the opportunities for publishing and selling eBooks are almost endless, and the cost to publish an eBook can be absolutely nothing. That's right. It can cost you ZERO dollars to publish an eBook. The biggest barriers to writing and publishing books have been removed with the no-cost eBook publishing. Amazon, who purchased Createspace, will also publish your book in PRINT for no cost to you! There is really nothing stopping you from participating in and profiting from the new self-publishing economy and paradigm. I will show you, step-by-step, how to write, publish, and ultimately profit from simple non-fiction books that are laser targeted to customers that will love your work, and perhaps buy everything that you write and produce.

Making the Mental Transition

There is a saying that everyone has a book inside them. When it comes to step-by-step books, it is much more likely that everyone has at least six books inside of them. How could that be, you ask? Think about the things that you are good at. What do people come to you for help with? What hobbies do you have? What interests and passions do you have? What associations are you a part of? What do you do for a living? What do you want to learn? It maybe that you can create your step-by-step eBook while you are learning something that you have wanted to learn for years. I personally prefer books written by people who openly admitted that they started from square one (actually everyone does start from square one, you just don't hear about it), then they summarized what it took to find the information that they needed and what it took to become proficient at whatever they are teaching.

What stops most people from creating a book or a product is not knowing how to start and the simple fear of getting out of their comfort zone to do it. In this eBook I am going to show you one step at a time how easy it is to create simple one problem-one solution, step-by-step, information eBooks that will really help other people, and will create a long-lasting income stream for you, the eBook creator

You can't stop at just creating the book however, as the book publisher, you will also need to learn a little book marketing. I will touch on some things that will help you promote your book and get it into the hands of lots of people. The beauty of this system is that it is the secret that moves people from just being authors to being creators and entrepreneurs. This day and age is the day and age of the authorpreneur. Someone who can create a book, easily publish it, and get it into the hands of people who desperately need it. Making that leap is as easy as putting your ideas on paper, doing some simple self-publishing, then using a little social media to help spread the word. Included are some tips for getting reviews, posting blog articles, and promoting yourself and your creative art as a writer.

Among the myths of eBook writing is the thought that an author must be an expert of some kind. This is false. A writer does have to have more knowledge than his ideal customer. If the customers weren't looking for additional knowledge than they already have, there would be no reason for the book. But a book can be interesting and informative if it contains just a few critical things:

1. That the information offered is accurate and useful.

2. That the information contained is relevant to the title and description, that it fully covers the promises made by the description material or the sales page.

3. That the information actually solves the problems that the reader bought it to solve!

That really is all there is to it. Anyone can write an eBook, and this book will help you do just that, one simple step at a time.

Providing What They Want and Need

There is no substitute for really knowing and understanding your customer. If you have experienced the problems that you write about, then you can identify with the feelings that your potential customers have felt or are feeling. Write about those feelings and make that emotional connection to the people that you want to help. There is an old saying that people don't care what you know, until they know how much you care. As an author, you can be a super-hero, you can make a difference in people's lives, but you have to help them know that you really understand them, that you get them. I find that good examples, stories, pictures, and simple instructions really help to make that connection.

In this eBook, I give you complete and direct, step-by-step instructions. I give you screenshots and working examples of how to research, compile, and quickly write your simple, step-by-step eBook that will really solve people's problems. My desire is to give you everything that you need to write your first step-by-step eBook, or teach you how to quickly get out your next book in a simple, straightforward, and very efficient manner.

Chapter 1: Choosing a Topic

The number of sales your eBook will make will depend on a number of things, not the least of which is choosing a topic that is of interest to a good number of people. As I have discovered myself, choosing the right topic can make the difference between many sales of your eBook, and just a few or none.

Criteria for Choosing a Topic

A good topic to write about normally has the following characteristics:

1. Lots of interest.
2. Some similar works that sell.
3. Something that you have knowledge about.
4. Something that you are passionate about.

Let's look at each of those criteria individually.

Lots of Interest

You can write a book about any subject, but if there isn't much interest in it, there won't be any sales. That is why a little bit of up-front research can make a whole lot of difference on the back-end profits.

What topics have a lot of interest? I have read numerous times that the "evergreen" topics are the ones to write about. Evergreen topics are those topics that have new people discovering an interest in the topic all of the time. This insures that there are always lots of brand new participants in the field. It also means these topics have many solutions, and that new solutions are ever evolving. So the term evergreen refers to both the participants around the topic, and the topic itself being renewed continually. Topics like this will naturally have lots of passionate people attracted to the topic, and will naturally have some controversy, because some solutions will work for some people and may not work for others. The characteristics of a topic that will insures that it has lots of interest are the following;

1. Lots of people suffering from the problem.
2. Lots of possible solutions.
3. People passionate about one or more solutions.

A list of the most common topics with lots of interest are the following:

Evergreen Topics

1. Health
2. Wealth
3. Self Help
4. Relationships

Does that mean that anything outside of those topics aren't good? Not at all, Chris Anderson, author of "The Long Tail" contends that there is a market for pretty much anything, but the smaller the pool of perspective customers, the fewer the sales are going to be.

If you need some inspiration about topics to write about, here are my suggestions for exploring some possibilities:

1. TV -- As the commercials come up while watching your favorite shows, just jot down what they were about and what problems the products being advertised are designed to solve. Is there a problem that interests you? It can be assumed that any problem mentioned on TV commercials have a significant amount of interest. If they did not, the companies sponsoring the advertisement would not be able to pay for it for very long.

2. Magazines – If you receive a magazine of some sort, search through it for the advertisements. Just like for television, what ads jump out at you? What ones pique your interest? The articles in the magazine can also be used to determine a topic. Usually the stories won't make it into the magazine unless there is sufficient subscriber interest. If you don't receive any magazines, simply stop at your local grocery store's magazine isle. Plan to spend a half an hour, and bring something to take notes.

3. The Library – Take a visit to your local library. Browse through the stacks of non-fiction books. Which titles jump out at you? What sections seem to be the biggest? Those books are a good representation of what your local community finds interesting. If some books never get checked out, they tend to lose their place to those that are more popular.

4. Google – Google has a tool called the Keyword Planner. It is a part of their Adwords suite of tools, so you have to have an account to use it, however, opening an account is free. You can find the tool here: https://adwords.google.com/ko/KeywordPlanner/Home . If you need some help using the tool, you can check out one of my other books here: http://www.amazon.com/ dp/B00E45ADKE/ .

Just know that you can enter search terms into the tool and get statistics about how often that word or phrase is searched on Google. This doesn't tell you if the search term is a good one for creating a book that will sell, but it does tell you if the topic has interest. Google also has a tool called Google trends, where it charts how search terms are doing over time, and will show which ones are increasing in interest or decreasing. You can find Google Trends here: www.google.com/trends/

5. Social Media – Facebook, Twitter, YouTube, LinkedIn and many, many more social sites have conversations running on them all of the time. You may get ideas with regards to what topics to write about by visiting PageData for Facebook, at this URL -- http://www.pagedatapro.com/pages/leaderboard/fc /fan_count . If you have a twitter account, trends can be accessed everyday from your account on the left column. For YouTube, trends can be monitored from the trends dashboard: http://www.youtube.com/trendsdashboard .

6. Book Sellers – Amazon, Barns and Noble, Smashwords, etc. Pull up one or more of these sites. Before you even put in a search term or do anything to influence what you are being shown, look at the advertisements. What do you see? You see books that are popular! You see the exact words that book sellers use to get your attention. Write down what jumps off of the page at you. Those should be some great topics to research!

Try to choose a subject that you think will have interest now and, in the future, be careful with fads where the interest mushrooms now, then disappears over time, however, being one of the first ones to write about new topics can be very lucrative.

Chapter Two: Similar Works That Sell

Now that you have a topic, you will need to narrow down the topic to one problem – one solution. Narrowing your focus to one problem will do a number of things for you. It will make the book more focused, it will make the book more specific to an exact set of customers, but it will also make the book much easier to write. This type of book shouldn't cover the entire history of a topic, it shouldn't need hundreds of pages, it shouldn't ramble or be full of fluff material, this type of book is right-to-the-point and delivers specific and needed information about one specific problem and how to solve that problem—that is it.

The question is how to narrow down the topic, and still write about something that will have enough interest to sell. Well, it is time to do a little analysis. The best way to know whether a book will sell is to look at others like it that might be selling. There is a mistaken theory that if there is competition out there, your book won't sell. The truth is that competition, in this case, is a good thing. It means that people are interested in the subject, and are buying books around that subject.

Think about books that you own or have checked out of the library. Do you only read one book ever on one particular subject? Not very likely, you read several books on the topic, because the topic interests you, and because you might want to see what suggestions come from multiple people with different perspectives. You will want to differentiate your book from the competition, but you want to see a number of books that are selling about your general topic, and one or two that kind of cluster around your narrow subject.

We're going to start with Clickbank. Clickbank is a market place for digital products. Those products are mostly information products that can be sold by affiliates. Affiliates are people who help advertise on their own web pages, blogs, or social media, who receive a portion of the purchase price. Clickbank is a good place to do research, because they provide some analytics about what is selling, and the authors of the eBooks tend to put a lot of time creating a sales page for the eBook that tells us a LOT about the book. The Clickbank marketplace can be accessed here: https://accounts.clickbank.com/marketplace.htm .

Research on Clickbank

1. Go to the Clickbank Marketplace URL (https://accounts.clickbank.com/marketplace.htm)
2. Click on the Advanced Search link

3. Select Gravity "Higher Than", insert the number 20.
4. Type in your topic at the search bar.
5. Scroll down through the list of products.

You can see the Clickbank Market place in figure 1, and the list of products the search produces in Figure 2.

Figure 1, Clickbank Marketplace Advanced Search

Displaying results 1-10 out of 54 (pg. 1 of 6)

Results per page: 10 ▼

Sort results by:
Keyword Relevance ▼

Eat Stop Eat- The New Expanded Version!

Avg $/sale

Double The Length, With New Chapters On Hunger, Resistance Training
And Weight Training! The Leading On-line Book On Flexible Intermittent
Fasting Just Got Even Better. People Love This Book For A Reason!

$34.31

PROMOTE

Vendor Spotlight

Stats: Initial $/sale: $19.47 | Avg %/sale: 75.0% | Avg Rebill Total: $24.31 | Avg %/rebill: 75.0% |
Grav: 56.67
Cat: Health & Fitness : Diets & Weight Loss

The Carb Nite Solution (view mobile)

Avg $/sale

The Carb Nite® Solution Is Not Another Lifestyle Diet. The Carb Nite®
Solution Is An Advanced Diet Plan Designed To Strip Body Fat Safely,
Rapidly And Permanently.

$14.20

Stats: Initial $/sale: $14.20 | Avg %/sale: 50.0% | Grav: 33.91
Cat: Health & Fitness : Diets & Weight Loss

Figure 2, List of eBooks on Clickbank

What you see in this list are the eBooks that correspond to your topic which have a gravity score of 20 or more. Gravity is a unique metric used by Clicbank that more or less denotes the number of separate affiliates that are credited to have sold that particular eBook during a specific period of time. It doesn't really equate directly to sales of the eBook, but it is the most commonly used metric to compare the performance of one eBook over another on Clickbank. A gravity of 20 or more is respectable, so those are the products you want to look at.

Are there a number of eBooks that show up? Are there any eBooks with gravity over 100? If there are eBooks in the list, which would mean that there are products with a gravity of over 20, then there are books on that topic that are selling. If there are eBooks or products with a gravity of over 100, then that means there is a book or product that is selling very well.

You might want to try entering other words that might also describe your major topic. For example, if your topic was "weight loss", you might try "shed pounds", "eat healthy", "exercise", or any other similar term you can come up with. If you find a general term that has fewer overall books in the category, but the gravity of the books on average seems to be higher, you might make a note of that subject, and focus on that sub area of the topic.

Another tool for sorting Clickbank products by popularity is the CBEngine.Com Tool.

1. Go to CBEngine.Com.

2. Input your main topic into the search bar on the left, and click on Search.
3. View the list of products that are returned.

Actually, finding the search bar is not intuitive. You need to go to the left column to find it. Below is a screen shot that might help you.

Figure 3, CBEngine front page

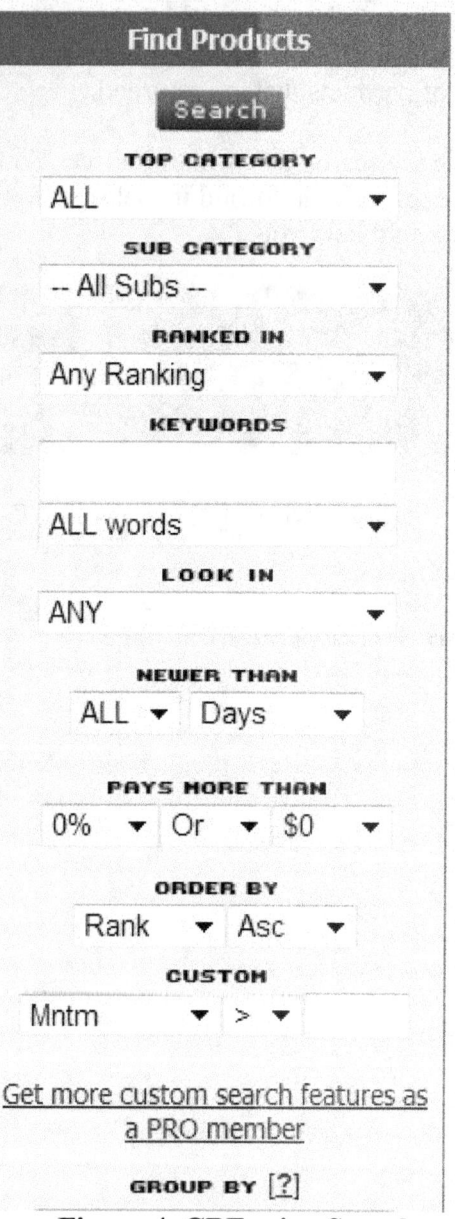

Figure 4, CBEngine Search

Amazon Research

Amazon is the biggest online eBook marketplace in the world. A quick check on Amazon can tell you a lot about books that are out there and are selling.

1. Go to the Amazon marketplace. (Amazon.com)
2. In the search bar, click on the down arrow, and select Kindle Store.
3. Type in your topic, and click on Go.
4. In the showing results tab, select image, this will give you a screen full of titles.
5. Change the sort by selection to New and Popular. Click Go.

Figure 5, Selections for Searching On Amazon

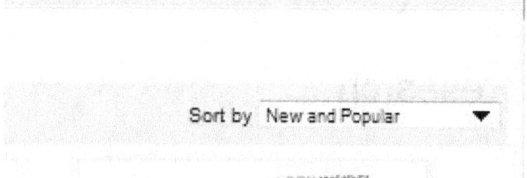

Sort by New and Popular ▼

LOOK INSIDE!

Figure 6, One More Amazon Modification

Now you should have a list of the best sellers for your topic. The book listings should appear in a grid fashion so that you can compare titles and covers very easily. The grid should appear as shown in Figure 7.

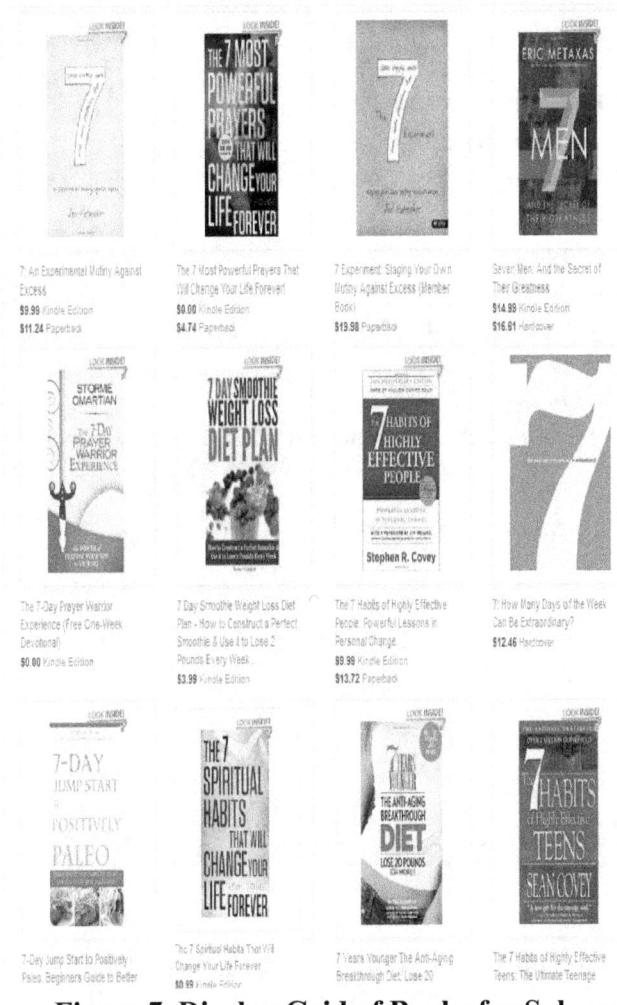

Figure 7, Display Grid of Books for Sale on Amazon

Click on individual books. Look at the product details for several of the books, display of the product details is shown in Figure 8.

Product Details

File Size: 5069 KB

Print Length: 392 pages

Publisher: Putnam Adult; 1st edition (January 6, 1997)

Sold by: Penguin Group (USA) LLC

Language: English

ASIN: B00256Z2HI

Text-to-Speech: Enabled ☑

X-Ray: Enabled ☑

Lending: Not Enabled

Amazon Best Sellers Rank: #10,165 Paid in Kindle Store (See
        #47 in Kindle Store > Kindle eBooks > Health, Fitness & Die

Figure 8, Details of eBook on Amazon

Are there a few books there that have an Amazon
Bestsellers Rank of 20,000 or less? If so, this is
probably a good topic to write about.

What is Amazon Bestsellers Rank?

There are millions of books in the Amazon Kindle
Store. Amazon ranks each one from the top seller,
with an Amazon Bestsellers Rank of 1, to the very
least seller with an Amazon Bestsellers Rank that
could be a few million.

I have found a number of charts that map sales of Kindle eBooks to their sales rank. I like this one from Theresa Ragan, https://www.theresaragan.com/salesrankingchart .

The numbers below are based on indie authors who have been willing to share their numbers.

Amazon Best Seller Rank 100,000+ - selling less than one book a day.
Amazon Best Seller Rank 50,000 to 100,000 - selling close to 1 book a day.
Amazon Best Seller Rank 10,000 to 50,000 - selling 3 to 15 books a day.
Amazon Best Seller Rank 5,500 to 10,000 - selling 15 to 30 books a day.
Amazon Best Seller Rank 3,000 to 5,500 - selling 30 to 50 books a day.
Amazon Best Seller Rank 500 to 3,000 - selling 50 to 200 books a day.
Amazon Best Seller Rank 350 to 500 - selling 200 to 300 books a day.
Amazon Best Seller Rank 100 to 350 - selling 300 to 500 books a day.
Amazon Best Seller Rank 35 to 100 - selling 500 to 1,000 books a day.
Amazon Best Seller Rank 10 to 35 - selling 1,000 to 2,000 books a day.
Amazon Best Seller Rank of 5 to 10 - selling 2,000 to 4,000 books a day.
Amazon Best Seller Rank of 1 to 5 - selling 4,000+ books a day.

This is an old chart that I am leaving as an example of how rankings used to work. The numbers are different today because of borrows and kindle unlimited. The Kindlepreneur has a ranking calculator that is a little more accurate. You can find it here: https://kindlepreneur.com/amazon-kdp-sales-rank-calculator/

These may change over time as more and more books make their way into the Amazon market place.

Writing with Knowledge

As I mentioned initially, you don't have to be an expert or have spent 10,000 hours on any subject to be able to write about it. You do have to have some solid information, however. Writing is easier when it is about things that you already have some working knowledge about. Having said that, you can write a good book about a subject that you have an interest in and are willing to do some research on.

Here are some places that you can do some low-cost to no-cost research:

1. Search Engines – Google it. Use search engines to discover overall topics, but more importantly use it to find the best resources. Look at information on sites like Wikipedia. Look for the biggest authority sites on the web around your topic, and see what information they have about your topic. Search for blogs on your topic by typing your topic + blog into the Google search field.

2. Visit the Library – There may be books at your local library on the subject, and there may be magazines at the library that you can reference while you are there.

3. Visit Forums – The most active and passionate people talking about your topic often congregate on forums. Search for forums about your topic by typing your topic + forum into the Google search field. Register for the forum and spend a little time there. Make comments about other people's posts, create posts of your own, and ask questions. There may be a number of experts that do visit the forum, and perhaps they will have the kind of advice that you want to share with your readers.

4. Visit the Amazon Kindle Store – Set the sort by field to "Low to High". You might find some eBooks that are on free promotion for the day, or you may be able to find a number of eBooks that sell for 99 cents to $2.99. That is a great value for research material. Other places that occasionally have discounted books are Smashwords, Barnes and Noble, and Kobo.

Writing with Passion

Write about the things that you have a real interest in. Nothing is harder than sitting down to a blank screen trying to come up with what to say, when you have a topic that bores you. I would so much rather read something from someone that is excited about his or her subject, than from someone who doesn't have any passion about the object of their writing.

Spend a little time coming up with possible topics to write about. Here are the questions that you should be asking yourself.

1. What do people come to you for help with?
2. What do you do at work that you could help people do?
3. What hobbies do you have that you can teach people about?
4. Do you have any pets? What could you teach people about taking care of your pets?
5. What problems have you solved in your family or life that you could help other people through?

Make a list of the answers to the above questions. Which ones do you believe would make a good book?

Create a file or a notebook where you write down every good idea for a book that you come across. Over time you will have a pretty good list. That list will help you keep coming up with good book ideas. Don't cross any of the ideas off, just find a way to mark ideas as ones you want to work on now, or those you want to put off until later.

Chapter 3: A One Problem One Solution Book

Now you are at a point where you have thought about your topic and have done a little bit of research to know that the topic is one that has lots of interest, and books that are selling. The hardest part of this process is narrowing the topic to one problem, one solution.

What might be the biggest problems in your niche or about your topic that you can solve? Here are the best ways to determine that:

1. When you visit forums, sort the threads by the ones with the most views and/or most replies. These will typically deal directly with the subjects that people on the forum are the most concerned about.

2. When you visit Clickbank, don't just browse through the list of products, go ahead and open up the links to the sales pages. On each sales page of the products that are relevant to your topic, go through the introduction to the product. What problems are being addressed by this eBook or product? Write down, in your own words, the problem or problems that are being addressed. Add these to the list of books that you could write.

Now pay particular attention to the list of benefits, the bullet-points in the sales letter. Each of those bullet-points could make a book in and of its self, or are there two, three or four that could be combined into something cohesive surrounding one problem? The copywriters that create sales pages often understand exactly what people are looking for, and the emotional triggers to get them to buy. If you can glean the major ideas from the copywriting on the sales page, then you have perfect subjects to write about.

3. While you are on Amazon, scan through the covers and titles of the eBooks that come up in your search about your topic. Write down the ones that seem interesting to you, or write down a whole page of the "New and Popular" titles. Now, here is your chance to be creative:

A. Can you change the title just a little bit to emphasize some other aspect of the topic?

B. Can you address a different set of people? Or address the same set of people in a different way?

C. Can you see a hole in what has been covered by the other eBooks? What subjects have been left out?

D. Can you see a better way to describe a subject covered by one or more of the books?

E. Do any of the book covers or titles give you ideas about books that you haven't considered before?

If you are still on Amazon.com, then click on the icon representing a book cover. Now click on the "Look Inside" feature. Scroll down to the Table of Contents. The table of contents is a list of chapter headings. Each chapter heading could make a book in and of itself. Which chapters do you see that you could do a "deep dive" on and expand it into a whole book, or are there two or three chapters that could be combined to make one book? The information here is pure gold, and should give you plenty of new ideas for directions to go with your book.

Chapter 4: Creating Your Book

Writing a book can be fun and exciting. If it feels like going to the dentist, then you are doing it wrong! Some of the things that you should keep in mind are:

1. Write like you are speaking to a friend. Try to write your book as if you were talking to a friend. I will often think about someone I know that I believe would like to learn more about the subject that I will be writing about. I picture that person in my mind, and then just try to imagine having a conversation with that person. I try to think of the questions he or she might have and how best to answer those questions for them specifically. I have heard of other writers that write down characteristics of their ideal customer. Then they search through pictures from Google images of someone that they think could represent that group. They blow up the picture to an 8x10 and post it on their wall. When they write, they refer to the picture.

2. Be yourself. Find your own style. In authorship we refer to this as voice. Find your own voice, people who read your work and like it, will like it because of your unique voice. They may become a fan of yours, and buy every book that you put out. This can't happen if you are trying to copy or be someone else. Just be yourself, and you will advance your author platform faster than anything else you can do.

3. Research and read the things that you love. In fact, copy the table of contents from the books that you love, write the introductions and sales pages out by hand word for word. Don't ever include any of this copied work in your books, (that would be plagiarism) but as you copy, the information becomes engrained into your mind and becomes a part of you. As you think about it, and try to reproduce it, you will be able to deliver that information in your own words and in the ways that you understand it best.

4. Finally, write the book that you want to read. I have read that most advice is rhetorical in nature, it is what someone would have said to an earlier version of him or herself. Write your book of "advice" to yourself. What do you wish you had known years ago? How do you wish it would have been packaged and presented? What examples can you give from your own personal life or from the lives of those whom you know or love that would keep others from making the same mistakes or could help others move along more quickly than you were able to?

The Structure of Your Book

We all have certain expectations. When it comes to books, we all expect that there won't be any typos and that grammar mistakes will be at a minimum. Getting help editing your book is one of the pieces of advice that I whole-heartedly suggest. I will provide some low to no-cost solutions near the end of the book for help editing your book, but realize that the expectations are there for any book to be of high quality. Typos and grammar mistakes are usually signs of non-professionalism, and can kill people's perception of your book. You can solve this one huge problem for your book by either hiring some professional editing services, or by crowd-source editing, which I will explain later. You can get some of these services for a reasonable price, but you have to be selective about where you get them.

When it comes to non-fiction books, where problems and solutions are presented, there are a few other formatting expectations. Usually a non-fiction books will have a format that loosely follows this example:

Introduction
Topic
       Subtopic
       Subtopic

.

.

.

Topic
       Subtopic

Subtopic

.

.

.

Conclusion

Your book should include at least three major topic and three subtopics for each topic. But it could contain many more. It is suggested that each topic have at least three main-points in them but could have four to six. If you topic or subtopic has more than six main points, then some of those should be broken out into a new topic.

Here are some ideas about what should be in the sections:

Introduction: The introduction talks about the problem and tries to make a connection with the reader. It can talk about the pain of the problem being suffered, and about where the problem can lead if it is not corrected. The introduction can also mention briefly the idea of how the problem can be solved and the benefits of solving the problem.

Topic One: Give a little bit of the background of the problem. Is this a problem you have experienced directly, or is it a problem that someone you know has experienced? How has this problem impacted their lives?

Topic Two: The Proposed Solution and why it will solve the problem.

Topic Three: Here is the piece that will make this book. Include the step-by-step instructions along with screen shots, pictures, examples, and details that will help your reader follow the directions to the tee.

Topic Four through topic N (however many you might need): Discuss any of the things to watch out for, gotchas that might crop up, or common things that people do wrong. Discuss any other tips or tricks that will make following the instructions easier, or provide better results. Discuss how to measure the success of what the reader should be doing. Encourage the reader to take immediate action. Create a list of resources that they might need, include software, books, materials and/or other references. Point out examples and/or case studies. Discuss places your readers can go to, or explore for further reading.

Conclusion: Summarize what has already been discussed concentrating on the final, overall, concise, 1, 2, 3, etc. steps. Finish with a strong call to action, and a final reminder of the big benefit of solving the problem.

This should complete your book! That really is it. Putting out your first eBook, or putting out the next eBook should be a very simple thing from here.

Chapter 5: Organizing a Book

I have used mind maps to organize ideas. They work well for me, especially when I am working on books with multiple aspects of a topic. I find, however, with one-problem, one-solution books, that I am more productive if I go right to writing a book outline. My template for the outline is something like this:

Topic Title

Introduction
Problem Topic
    Include the what, why, and who.
Solution Topic
    Give a detailed description of the solution and why it works.
Step-by-Step Topic
    Include all of the tools needed and how to use them.
What to Watch Out for Topic
    Include common misperceptions and myths.
More Tips and Trick Topic
Conclusion

Sprinkle the whole thing generously with examples, stories, quotes, or other proofs. Add illustrations and screenshots. Shoot for at least 5000 words. If you are going to release on Amazon, it is even better if you can get 10,000 to 15,000 words.

Creating a 6,000-word eBook can be broken down into the following time-line.

16 Days from Start to Finish

Day	Activity
1	Research Topic
2	Research Selling Potential
3	Create Outline, Organize Notes, Create the Sales Page
4	Write Introduction (500 to 1000 words)
5	Begin Chapter 1 (Problem Topic) (500 to 1000 words)
6	Finish Chapter 1 (Complete Problem Topic) (another 500 to 1000 words)
7	Begin Chapter 2 (Broad Solution Topic) (500 to 1000 words)
8	Finish Chapter 2 (Why the Solution Works) (another 500 to 1000 words)
9	Begin Chapter 3 (Step-by-Step Instructions for Solution) (500 to 1000 words)
10	Finish Chapter 3 (Complete Instructions) (Another 500 to 1000 words)

11   Begin Chapter 4 (What to Watch Out for Topic) (500 to 1000 words)
12   Finish Chapter 4 (Tips and Measuring Success) (Another 500 to 1000 words)
13   Write Conclusion (500 to 1000 words)
14   Edit book or outsource the editing.
15   Create cover art work or outsource it.
16   Publish book, put it up for sale, celebrate.

This is the ideal calendar that I would shoot for. I usually take weekends off. I will usually have multiple subtopics in each of my chapters, I will spend a day on each subtopic. I usually have more than four chapters and three or more subtopics in each topic. Each additional subtopic adds two days. Usually this brings the total word-count to somewhere between 20,000 and 50,000 words. At about 1000 words per day, that roughly equates to 20 to 50 ideal days to write my books. Keep in mind that I have a "day" job, so writing is something that I do an hour or so per day.

Breaking the work up like this insures that I get things done. Anyone can write 500 to 1000 words in an hour or two. There is also the possibility of outsourcing the work of writing, by breaking your outline up into chapters and hiring someone at Fiverr.com or Odesk.com to write a 1200-word to 1500-word article per chapter. Each article should cost around five dollars.

As for creating the cover art: You can have this outsourced as well, keep the cost under $30. If you want to try Fiverr.com, where you could get the cover made for five dollars, you may want to commission three different artists to see which one you like best, or to have a few to choose between.

There are some free options: if you have Photoshop or some other graphics program, you could attempt the cover. I would suggest that you pull up other covers on Amazon about your topic, and find a cover to model. The cover can make or break the sales of your book, so think hard about how you will handle getting the cover done. If you are going to do the cover yourself and you need photographs or artwork for your cover you can try us.creativecommons.org (pay particular attention to the license of the art work—not all of it can be used commercially), or paid art from dreamstime.com or istockphoto.com.

The Step-by-Step Parts

Writing instructions can really be an art. I like to put my instructions in a numbered list. Step one, step two, step three, and so on. I try to write the first draft of the instructions in a single sitting and without editing or checking on the steps. Then I go through the instructions a line at a time, and edit the steps and points that I might have left out or got incorrect in the second and third drafts. I draw up the final instructions, and hand them to a friend or associate that will go through them and try them out. If they have any questions, or if they can't follow the instructions very well, I get them to help me change the instructions so that they are easy to follow.

If you sit down and try to do the instructions as you write about them, you will usually end up missing things or jumping steps. If you write down the steps as you remember them, then edit the steps, you are less likely to forget something by being distracted while doing the steps and writing about them at the same time.

Writing Fast

If there is one strategy that will help any author, it is to put out more books. Sean Platt, the co-author of *Write. Publish. Repeat.* built his book around the concept that being successful as a writer requires putting more books on your personal bookshelf. Not only does the adage hold true that the more books you have for sale, the more sales you are going to have, but if you create a quality product, people that buy one of your books may become true fans of yours and buy the rest of your books as well. Each of your books can become a new "salesman" for your work. If they do a good job, people reading one book will come back for another of your books. Be sure to put as much love and quality into each book as you possibly can.

A good strategy is to create six or so books in a series. Make the first one free, then sell the others at $2.99. Package the set of the first three and sell them for $4.99, also package the last three and sell them for $4.99. Finally package the entire set for $8.99. That gives you three more "books" to add to your catalogue, but it also entices people to make a purchase of all of your books at one time, to save money.

I read once that most authors stop before they have published more than six books. Those that are successful, push past this number. If you can create those six books in a related niche, or in a series, the above strategy will push you past the six-book glass ceiling and put you squarely on the path to success as an author.

Create an Outline

The secret to writing faster is to have what you are going to write well outlined. Rachel Aaron, the author of *2000 to 10,000: How to Write Faster, Write Better, and Write More of What You Love*, takes readers on a journey of how she moved from two thousand words per day to ten thousand words per day on a consistent basis. Her big breakthrough happened when she took ten minutes before writing to create an outline of what her scenes were going to look like. She knew before she started typing what she was going to write, and it improved her performance considerably.

I put her strategy to the test, and found that it works for me. I now spend time everyday working on my outlines. When I have something complicated to work on, I will often start my outlines with a mind map. A mind map is just a tool, however. It gives me a way to view my subject as more of a whole.

I also like to use 3x5 cards and sticky notes to write my notes on. I will visit the library, or read through my books of research with 3x5 cards on my desk. I will write my notes on the cards, and write the reference to where I found the information. When I am ready to start writing my book, I spread the 3x5 cards and sticky notes all over my desk and wall. I use the cards to create my outline, and any time that I come to lull in my writing, I will take a few minutes to look over some of the notes spread out all over. Usually one or more will jog my memory, and help the ideas flow forward.

The computer is a wonderful tool, but touching physical things such as cards, sticky notes, physical books, and often my journal, helps super-charge my creativity. Creating a book can feel more like play than like work when you involve more of your physical senses.

Use a Mind Map

As I explained earlier, a mind map can be a great tool.
I like how easy it is to add topics or rearranged them
in a mind map. The mind map gives me a visual view
of everything that pertains to a certain topic. I can
sometimes divide the mind map in half, saving half of
the topics for a later book, then spreading the current
topics out over a new mind map. I use a free tool
called XMind for my mind map needs. I find,
however, that sometimes the computer is confining,
and does not let me see everything that I need to see
to wrap my head around my subject.

Since the mind map is the most "creative" part of the
book, and it is also the part that will save you the
most time, speed up your writing the most, and keep
you focused the best, I like to put a bit of time into the
mind map. I have often taken a good mind map and
pulled a very good outline right out of the mind map.

I will often create my mind map on a very LARGE
piece of paper. I have a sketch pad with pages that are
18x24. I will tear out two to four pages of these out of
my sketch pad. I will begin with one page, and start in
the middle with my topic.
I will draw a line from the center circle with my topic,
out in any direction, then create a circle where I write
in a subtopic. Usually I will begin to draw lines
around the subtopic and start to fill in details, facts,
and notes that I think relate to that subtopic.

I use the "splat" method when I'm doing this, I just try to get as much down as I can.

Then I draw another line from the center topic circle to where I draw another circle and write the name of a second subtopic in the circle. Then I fill out circles around it that have the ideas, details, facts, etc. I keep doing this until I have everything that I can think of that is related to that topic on the paper.

Often, I will need to expand from just one page. I will tape a second page to the first one and continue filling it out.

I will leave the mind map on my wall for a week or two—adding new subtopics and sometimes rearranging. If I need to, I will add a third page.

At some point I will decide to start on my outline. I can usually take the main topic as the starting point and make a chapter out of each subtopic.

I use the notes around each subtopic as the paragraphs or sections that I will cover. Once I have done this, the outline is complete, and I will start writing the book.

This method works well for non-fiction, but I also find it useful for fiction. I try to group the characters or groups of characters together with their backstories and the plot sequences, the character flaws, what I want the characters to learn, etc. together. When I get done, I can often outline the novel and jump to the writing.

Chapter 6: Becoming a Better Writer

Stephen Covey, in his book The *Seven Habits of Highly Successful People*, tied up the loose ends of the book in a chapter called, *Sharpen the Saw*. His point was that you have to do things everyday to improve yourself and build new skills. Writing is no different.

Here are the things that I try to do every day so that I improve my craft as a writer.

1. Write every day. Write, write, write, write. It has been said, practice makes perfect. There is nothing that will improve your skill more than practicing your writing. When I am doing research for my books, I try to write my notes out by hand on 3x5 cards, or in a file on the computer. But I make sure that I write notes every day. I am always working on a couple of books. I write something in those books every day. I also try to take time every day to do a few exercises that I think help me with my chosen topics and subjects.

2. Youhji Yamamoto said, "copy, copy, copy, copy, at the end of the copy you will find yourself." I believe that the quote has a lot of merit. I pull up the table of contents from two or three books in my niche every day and spend 10 minutes copying the table of contents, or the book description, or the introduction. None of this copying ever makes it into my personal work—but I use these things as some of the notes that I create my books from. The secret is in the copying. As you copy, you become very familiar with the structure of successful tables of contents, you become familiar with what a good introduction looks like, and what a good book description looks like. The ideas and concepts become part of you, and help you write with a passion that is all your own. At the end of the copy, you have the chance to form your own opinions, draw your own conclusion, and package what you have read and practiced into something that is your own style and voice.

The secret is to choose the best books, learn from the masters and the thought leaders in your chosen topic or niche. Let them be your guide, and then you can be a guide for others. Seek first to learn, then to share. The knowledge of your niche will grow inside of you, and you will have lots to share.

3. Read every day. Read fiction, nonfiction, assembly instructions, cereal boxes, advertisements in magazines, blog posts, and questions on forums. Reading lets you take in the world around you, it lets you see and taste what the world is talking about. Set aside a half an hour per day to just do some reading. Let your mind be taken away to where ever that reading leads you. If you find a book that you like, or an author that you enjoy, then do some research. Look at the end of the book for the references or bibliography. Read the books that led the author that you admire to the book that you really enjoyed reading by that author. It's not where you take the information that you learned from, it is where that information takes you, and where YOU take those ideas to. Start a journey that can bring you a lifetime of learning and enjoyment.

Writing Made Easy

Creating books on a consistent basis requires some work and discipline. I find the work a lot easier with some simple tools and organization. Here is a list of things that I use on a daily basis.

1. A file where I keep a list of potential book titles and/or topics and/or subjects. I try to keep a number out to the side of each item to let me know which ones I think are the highest priority, then I lump most of the rest of them into the lowest priority. The priorities change when I pull one off of the list to begin working on it, or when I feel differently about a subject and lower the priority on all of the line items related to that subject. Looking at this list often helps me prepare for the next few books that I want to work on.

2. A file of notes and references from other people's work, such as blog posts that I read, forum posts that I read and/or questions that I answer on forums. Notes from electronic books that I read, unless I decide to write the notes on 3x5 cards, and the names of mind maps and outlines that I am keeping on the topic or subject.

3. Mind map files. I try to keep mind maps on separate topics or subjects that I am thinking about or studying about, or might someday write about. I add to these files whenever I have a new idea, or run into a new idea in my research. I put short references to those ideas in my mind maps.

4. Book outlines. Some of the most important documents that I keep are outlines for my books. I start the outline a week or more before starting the book. I go through a few different ways of organizing the information, trying to address the most important issues and the biggest problems in the first chapters of the book. I keep changing and massaging these outlines until I have something that I think will work for an entire book. If I do a good job of the outline, the writing goes very smoothly. When the outline is weak, I will often have to do more rewriting than I care to admit.

5. A file with a list of important questions. When I get responses to my email or comments on my blog, or when I answer questions on forums, I try to keep those questions in a file related to each of my books. I try to answer all of the questions, or at least all of the important questions that I can with my book. I want the book to be beneficial and help a lot of people. When I am aware of the big questions around my topic, my book always does better.

Becoming a Bestseller

It is the dream of most writers to become a bestseller. The opportunity to be a New York Times bestseller is pretty limited, and very unlikely without the promotion of one of the big six publishers, but Amazon provides a continually updated list of their top 100 bestsellers as well as bestsellers in "every category".

Becoming a bestseller in one or more categories is very attainable by most any author. The ticket to becoming a category bestseller is helping Amazon sell more of your books. There are things inside of Amazon that you can do to promote your book and things outside of Amazon that you can do to promote your book. The next section of this book is about book promotion.

Promoting Your Books

The original model for selling books depended upon acquiring a publishing agent and the publisher trying to getting your book placed in a lot of libraries and bookstores. The publisher took on the major role of promoting your book. As a self-published author, you now have all of the book promotion to do yourself. I'm going to do all that I can to help you understand what you might be able to do to help promote your book.

Guy Kawasaki, and Shawn Welch, in their book *APE: Author, Publisher, Entrepreneur—How to Publish a Book*, explain that authors today have to be publishers and entrepreneurs as well. They have to take on the responsibility of publishing and promoting their library of books.

Being a Marketer

Most writers just want to write—they don't want to be bothered with marketing or promoting. It is easy to see why: don't you feel like you would just like to watch the Super Bowl without the interruptions of the advertisements? Don't you hate being interrupted with phone calls from pesky marketers? Interruptions aren't fun—so you don't want to be associated with those interruptions. Well, there are ways to get your book promoted without being a pesky marketer. First and foremost is to get everything that you can from Amazon. Amazon does a lot of book promotion for you, but it is kind of a catch 22. Amazon will promote your book, if it sells a lot of copies. Amazon puts your book in front of their customers in a number of ways.

1. By searches from search terms.
2. By category indexes.
3. By customers who bought this also bought list
4. Best Selling Lists

Chapter 7: Promoting on Amazon

Here are the things that you have some control and influence over concerning the Amazon platform. They include the cover, title, book description, categories, search terms, and reviews.

Cover

The cover is among the most important elements of what makes books sell on Amazon. The cover needs to look good at full size, but it also needs to look good at a thumbnail size as well. The title needs to be readable and the images recognizable at a very small size.

What should the cover look like? Browse over to Amazon.com, change the search type to Kindle Store. Type in a keyword for your topic--now look at the covers that impress you. What makes them jump off of the page at you? What makes them interesting or eye catching? Are there any elements that many of the covers share? How can you make your cover do something similar?

There are outsourcers that can create a cover for you for not much money. You could try Fiverr.com or Odesk.com to find them. Be sure to sort your searches by rating, and read the reviews posted by other customers. You really need to find the best outsourcers if you decide to go that route.

Title

The title is the next most important part of the equation. I like a title that is short and descriptive, containing keywords that are searched for often on the Amazon marketplace. The format for a nonfiction title should be Title: subtitle.

An example might be the following:
Funny Cats: Playful Cats, Sleeping Cats, and Cats We All Love

The topic would be cats. The title would be Funny Cats, the subtitle would be Playful Cats, Sleeping Cats, and Cats We All Love.

The Title Funny Cats should be in very large print on the front cover. The subtitle could be in small print below it, or at the bottom of the cover. The image should be a very funny cat picture.

What you type into the title field, however, needs to be the entire title, colon, subtitle. Everything in the title field is searchable, and can be used to find your book.

When you choose a title, think about this: How are people going to find my book? One of the ways is through the Amazon search field. Make sure that each portion of your title will help people find your book.

Book Description

The book description is the sales page for your book. Once someone is enticed by your cover and by your title, the next thing they are going to click on is the book description. What should be in the book description? The benefits of reading your book! Don't just make a quick summary of the book, create enticements for readers to buy the book. If the main problem that you are teaching people to solve is "remove acne", perhaps you could mention that following your step-by-step program, readers will enjoy the benefits of smooth and clear skin. If you are working on a recipe book, then the benefits would be children eating what is on their plate, and adults coming back for seconds. You might throw in that with these recipes, readers will never be embarrassed about having guests over to dinner. Look through the list of questions that your book addresses, and talk about the benefits of learning those lessons.

If you have other books that you have written on this topic, or specific credentials that make what you have to say in this book more meaningful, the book description is a place to put that kind of information. You have about 700 words that you can use in your description—be sure to use as many of those 700 words as possible. Get searchable keywords in the description as well, people might find your book because Amazon found something in the description that aligned with what one of their customers typed in the search bar.

Categories

There is a lot that can be said for the Amazon categories. The categories can be found on the right side of the Amazon search form when you select the Kindle Store and hit Go with no keywords in the search bar, then select Kindle eBooks.

New Releases
   Last 30 days (103,265)
   Last 90 days (283,935)
   Coming Soon (7,295)

Department
‹ Kindle Store

Kindle eBooks

Arts & Photography (141,699)

Biographies &
   Memoirs (109,339)

Business & Investing (148,532)

Children's eBooks (127,749)

Comics & Graphic
   Novels (23,725)

Computers &
   Technology (44,045)

Cookbooks, Food &
   Wine (35,877)

Crafts, Hobbies &
   Home (49,781)

Education &
   Reference (152,975)

Gay & Lesbian (23,881)

Health, Fitness &
   Dieting (150,808)

History (142,080)

Humor &
   Entertainment (57,222)

Literature & Fiction (739,431)

Mystery, Thriller &
   Suspense (133,376)

Figure 9, Kindle Categories

Figure 9 is a screen shot of what the kindle categories look like. Notice that each category has the number of eBooks in that category within the parenthesis. Clicking on a category will reveal a number of sub-categories below. People browse through the categories to find new books. You will want to experiment with the categories to discover which ones do the best for your book. For example, you may have a children's book that features family activities. You might find a couple of categories under Children's Books that seem to fit your book, but a little investigation may help you discover a category under Parenting and Relationships called Family Activities. This category may be smaller than the ones in the Children's Book section, and may afford you more views than the previous one. There may be a number of other categories that could be considered as well. The best one will only be discovered by you with a little bit of testing. One of the benefits of selling your eBook through Amazon is that the category your book is in can be easily changed and the change will show up within 24 hours.

Search Keywords

Amazon provides seven "Search Keyword" fields where you can enter up to seven search terms. Select these carefully, the search terms may determine how many people will find your book. Look for terms that are searched a lot on Amazon. One tip for doing this is type in a keyword for your topic then a space, you will see that Amazon suggests a number of terms below the search bar. Write down these terms, they might make good search terms to put in the Search Keywords field of your Amazon Kindle Direct Publishing book page. Figure 10 shows what the suggested terms look like.

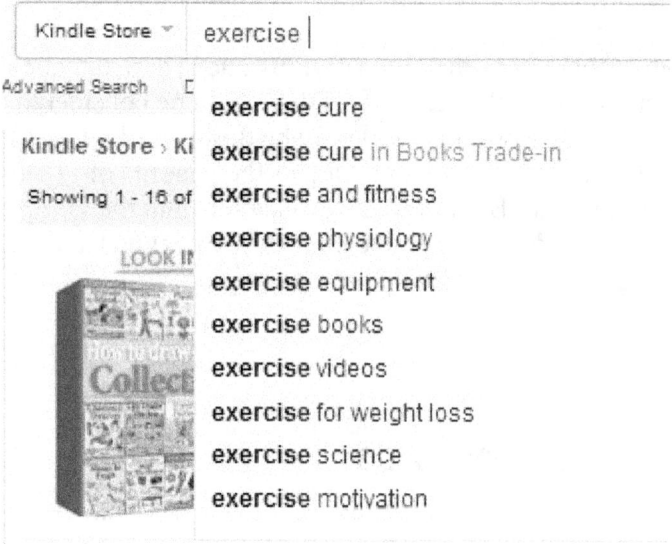

Figure 10, Amazon suggestion drop down

Search keywords along with the title and subtitle are the foundation for getting people to see your book on amazon, that you may want some automated help to find what you are going to put here. Dave Chesson, the Kindlepreneur, has created a product called KDP Rocket. It uses automation to help you find the most common terms used to search for different topics, and gives you some Amazon Analytics on how many people type those terms in. I have found the program very useful. If you want more information about it, you can see my blog post, http://austinsgift.com/KDPRocket.

Reviews

Have you ever made a purchase because of a recommendation from a friend? I have. Reviews posted on Amazon can influence the purchase decision of people who have found an interest in your book and are still deciding whether to purchase it. Using the Kindle Select program to set aside five days out of 90 days to put your book on a free promotion can get a lot of free copies in the hands of possible reviewers.

My personal advice is to combine your free day with some specific efforts to get reviews.

1. Make a list of people that you know that would be interested in the subject of your book then make a personal invitation to those people to download your book when it is free. Take time to follow up with them later, and ask them personally to post a review for you on Amazon.

2. At the end of this book I have a resource page where I list 20 or so Kindle Book Facebook groups. Join these groups and make a contribution to the discussions on occasion. Watch for people who announce their free days and request reviews of their free book. Download their free book, and post a review—not looking for anything in return, just to be active on the group and make sure that people in the group see your name and your contributions. When you have your free days scheduled, announce those free days and ask for reviews. People in the group will recognize your name, and if they have an interest in your subject will likely download your book and could leave you a review. The concept of a free book for an honest review is a time revered tradition. You are not soliciting "good" reviews, you are only asking for reviews in exchange for a free book.

3. Look at reviewers of books that are similar to yours. You may be able to follow up with those reviewers and offer them a free copy of your book to do a review.

4. Always ask for a review at the end of your book. Provide a link to your Amazon Sales Page so that readers only have to click one link to get to where they can leave you a review. People who liked your book just may take you up on your request.

There are a number of ways to get more reviews. Never pay for reviews, except for gifting or paying for a copy of your book for others to review. Paying for reviews is against Amazon's terms of service. Be an avid reviewer yourself, contact other authors in your genre or topic. People who buy one book on a topic, will often buy many books on the same topic. Other authors on your topic aren't necessarily competition, they can be partners in a way, by keeping people interested in the topic.

Creating an Email List

Getting your eBooks out on the Amazon platform can provide a pretty good income at this time, but platforms change over time. It is a really good idea to connect with your audience, to have your own blog, and have your own email list.

1. Invite people who read your book to get on your email list.

2. Invite people who visit your blog to get on your email list.

3. Set up an autoresponder with Aweber, GetResponse, or Mail Chimp.

4. Set up the autoresponder to send out an email once a week or so. Make sure that you let people know who you are, what you are trying to do with your books, and then send out broadcast emails to let them know about new books coming up or recent blog posts.

Ultimately, you want real fans that will follow you where ever your books are published, regardless of the platform. That is the power of having your own email list.

Creating an Author Platform

You need a blog as an author. You can start with a free one from Blogger or Wordpress.com, but consider purchasing hosting and buying a domain name that is your own. Post things about you, your writing, and new books that you put out. Post about tips and tricks around your topic, and be genuinely helpful. Give away some of your best information in your blog posts, and people will generally become more interested in buying your book.

1. Create an author profile at Amazon's Author Central

2. Create an author profile at Goodreads.

3. Create a Facebook fan page for your book

4. Create a twitter account.

These are ways to connect with your readers and create real fans. Answer questions and respond to comments, and you will see your fan base increase.

These activities are still secondary to writing more books. Set aside 20 minutes to half an hour every other day or so to do them, but don't let them steal from your writing time.

Creating eBook Funnels

Focus on writing more books. Each book has the potential to draw in new fans of your writing. People who like one of your books will be much more likely to buy more of them. This is how you create product funnels that siphon people a few at a time into your stream of income. The secret is, your books have to be good and your books have to solve a specific problem for a specific set of people. If they do that, a select set of people will love your books and buy more of them.

Chapter 8: Creatively Leveraging the Work of Giants

"If I have seen further than other men, it is because I have stood on the shoulders of giants." Isaac Newton exclaimed these words, and they hold true when it comes to writing. No man is an island when it comes to ideas that are popular. Success breeds success, if you want success you will need to look at successful models.

1. Write down a list of your favorite books and what made them endearing to you.

2. Look through the stacks at the library, and search through Amazon for books that you might like to read.

3. Answer these questions in a file or on a 3x5 card:
What do the books that appeal to you have in common?
What makes them stand out to you?
What makes you pick up a title to look closer at it?

Those elements are the ones you want to build on. They should be at the center of your writing and what you create. Now that you have the firm foundation to work with, you can begin to customize your work and make it uniquely yours.

What Would I Expect to Find?

Unlock your inner creativity and teach yourself to be working outside of the box with the following exercises:

1. When you open a book, open first to the table of contents.

2. Write down the table of contents one line at a time.

3. Now write a sentence about what you would expect to find in each chapter or section outlined in the table of contents of the book you just opened.

4. Browse through the chapters and compare. How close were the thoughts that you wrote down to what the author had to say?

5. Keep that list as notes to the book you are writing. Even if your thoughts didn't match that of the author, they will probably still make good ideas to write about in your own book.

6. Create Your Own Table of Contents

Now shut the book, and create a table of contents that you think would cover the subject. First of all, just put down a list of subjects that you would cover if you were writing the book. Next arrange that list in a way that makes sense. Why would you talk about one subject before the other? Why would you include one thing instead of a different one? This could be the basis for the outline of your next book.

What Was Left Unsaid?

My father owned some apartments, and as a youth, I became very acquainted with carpentry and plumbing. One of the tasks that I ended up doing on a few occasions was installing tile. I was always amazed at how rough and uneven the floor would be before we started the tile installation. We took a compound that we put over the floor that filled in all of the gaps and the uneven parts so that the tile could be placed perfectly on top.

Most books are like the floor, they often provide a frame work, and some great super-structures here and there, but they often leave little gaps and holes. As you read other books about the topics you are studying, look for areas that are not covered well. These make great opportunities for expanding on the work of others, and adding important points of your own.

How Would I Make it Better?

Have you ever finished a book and thought that you liked it OK, but it could have been a whole lot better? Here is the chance for you to write the book that you want to read. Find the weak points of your competition's books, and shore those up. Make sure that you address the weak points, and let people know that your book doesn't leave out those important points.

Chapter 8: Publishing Your Book

I have talked a lot about publishing to the Amazon Kindle Direct Publishing platform. I have a number of books published there. I also have books published at other eBook publishing platforms. I get the most sales out of Amazon, and seem to get the most help promoting my books from Amazon. If you are new to self-publishing I would suggest starting there. Here is a link where Amazon walks you through the process of publishing your book. https://kdp.amazon.com/en_US/help/topic/G20063 5650 I feel they do a good job, and that I don't need to repeat their instructions in this book.

There is one gotcha that I want to mention. Sometimes formatting the book for Kindle can be a little tricky. Here is a free book, put out by Amazon that should help you with the formatting. http://www.amazon.com/Building-Your-Kindle-Direct-Publishing-ebook/dp/B007URVZJ6/ . I found it easier, however, to use a formatting service. I use KInstant Formatter. You can learn about KInstant formatter here => http://austinsgift.com/Kinstant-Formatter .

There are also other places you can publish to, including but not limited to:

Barnes and Noble
Apple iTunes
Smashwords
Kobo
Clickbank
JVZoo

And many others. Amazon also provides Print-On-Demand, now that they purchased Createspace, which means that you can get your book made into a physical book, and copies of the book sent out to customers as they buy it, one copy at a time.

Amazon also provides audio books through audible.com. That makes two other ways to get your book published for people to consume. If you enter into the Kindle Select program to use the 5 free days of promotion, you have to give Amazon exclusive rights to sell your book for 90 days. I would suggest doing the Kindle Select Program at least for the first 90 days to get those free days during which you can put a big effort into getting reviews for your book. Then you could consider expanding to other retailers.

Just Do It

Carrie Underwood once said, "Throw caution to the wind and just do it." That is the best advice that I can give you. Start today. Get your list of possible topics together. Spend a couple of hours getting that narrowed down to something that you want to write about, and just start doing it. All of the roadblocks that have held you back before will simply melt away as you sit down and just start typing.

Set a goal—shoot for writing 500 words every day. When you reach that on a consistent basis, set your goal for 1000 words every day. You will be surprised at how quickly you can get a 15,000 or 20,000-word nonfiction book written if you crank out a thousand words or more every day. If your topic is VERY specific, you can even get by with 5,000 to 10,000 words—but that would have to be very focused on a very specific issue and still has to address **everything** that it needs to cover. Step-by-Step books are very focused and specific by nature, and can usually be smaller by being much more specific about how EXACTLY to do something.

The Step-by-Step Checklist for Creating Your Book

Here is the checklist that I go through to produce a single step-by-step book.

Research
_____ 1. Extract a topic from your list of possible topics to write about.
_____ 2. Test the probabilities of having a good topic by checking on Clickbank and/or Amazon.
_____ 3. Narrow the topic to a more specific subject to write about.
_____ 4. Compile a list of questions gathered from question sites, forums, or gathered from sales pages or descriptions of other eBooks.

_____ 5. Find answers to those questions from multiple sources including, but not limited to forums, ezinearticles, other books, blogs, and authority sites.

_____ 6. Create notes from the research you have previously done include quotes from other book, ideas developed from the table of contents of other books, ideas from the descriptions or sales pages of other books. Get those ideas on 3x5 cards or in a mind map.

Organization

_____ 7. Lay out your notes, 3x5 cards, printed files of ideas, any other research around you.

_____ 8. Organize those notes and come up with a sample book outline.

_____ 9. Compare the book outline to other books available, do you include things not obviously found in one of the other books?

_____ 10. Come up with a book description or sales page. List all of the benefits that readers will get from following the step-by-step instructions you will provide.

_____ 11. Plan out step-by-step instructions. What subtopics will the instructions come into play with?

_____ 12. Design the overall step-by-step set of instructions.

Writing

_____ 13. Plan out when you will write. Most writers find it better to set aside the same hours every day.

_____ 14. Create a goal and a calendar. Plan on 500 words per day to begin with. Increase that number as you can.

_____ 15. Take five to ten minutes every day to plan out exactly what you will be writing about during the day.

_____ 16. Chart your progress. Mark whether you completed 500 words that day, came up short, or wrote even more.

_____ 17. Keep a file with the names of the sources for resources or a bibliography.

_____ 18. Edit your book. Read it over three times. Have multiple people read it over as well.

_____ 19. Consider hiring an editor.

Exercises

_____ 20. Take time every day to do a little reading, to practice copying tables of contents, book descriptions, and introductions.

Publishing

_____ 21. Create or outsource a killer cover.

_____ 22. Finalize your book title.

_____ 23. Research the Amazon categories you want to publish to.

_____ 24. Research the keywords you expect to use.

_____ 25. Put your book up for sale on Amazon Kindle Direct Publishing.

_____ 26. Get the link to your book, then modify your book to have the link in it and ask for reviews.

_____ 27. Consider publishing a physical book and an Audible audio file.

_____ 28. Schedule five free days on the Amazon Kindle Select program.

Marketing

_____ 29. Become a member of some or all of the eBook Facebook groups.

_____ 30. Complete your Author profile at Amazon's Author Central.

_____ 31. Get a profile at Goodreads.

_____ 32. Create a Facebook Fan Page for your book.

_____ 33. Create a twitter account for your book.

_____ 34. Contribute to the Facebook groups, especially those asking for reviewers.

_____ 35. List your free days with a number of websites that promote free Kindle books.

_____ 36. Ask for reviews while your book is free.

_____ 37. Make some posts to your blog and social media.

Repeat

_____ 38. Start your next book!

At first look it appears to be a lot of steps, but I have broken it down into very, very small individual steps that can be conquered one at a time. This is something that you can do so easily and so quickly. Just do it. Start today, you will never be sorry that you took the first step.

Conclusion

I hope that you have enjoyed this eBook. My desire is that it has helped you see that you can write an eBook, and that a simple step-by-step eBook could and should be one of the first ones that you write. There are so many things that you are good at, problems that you have personally solved or ones that you have solved for your business, organization, family, or friends. You may have hobbies that you would love to teach others more about, or other interests that you would love to share with others. Writing is truly about sharing, not about showing how smart you are, nor about proving anything to the world, it is simply sharing what is in your heart and what brings you joy.

Once you realize that your objective in writing is simply to share with others what you have learned or what you know, then writing becomes fun and exciting. There is no satisfaction as deep as the satisfaction that comes when you hear from others how your writing changed them for the better, how it helped them solve their problems, and how you contributed, even just a little bit, to their personal happiness.

Book reviews mean so much to independent authors. If you have enjoyed this book, I would like to invite you to leave a review on Amazon. You can leave the review here =>
http://www.amazon.com/dp/B00I0MKFVY, thank you SO much!

Now, make a goal today to start writing. Make a goal to have six books out by this time next year. That is a totally reachable goal. Break down what you have to do into tiny daily chunks, and just start doing it. You will be amazed at how quickly those little bits of writing become something significant. You cannot fail, you will be successful if you work on it every day, and if you don't give up.

Here is to your Ultimate Success,

Dean Giles

Bonus Just For You

Here is the First Chapter of the next book in this "How to Write a Book" series. The Book is called, "Discover Book Ideas."

Discover Book Ideas – Kindle Niche Book Ideas That Sell Books, Make Writing Faster, and Create Best Sellers

By Dean Giles

Introduction

Write in a Niche That Sells

"A journey of a thousand miles begins with a single step." -- Lao Tzu

The journey to writing a book that is popular begins with discovering a niche or topic that people are really interested in. That seems obvious, but few authors actually start where they need to. Just a little bit of research up front can explode sales on the back-end and make the writing worthwhile and fulfilling.

Self-publishing on Kindle has revolutionized the book market and has created opportunity for almost anyone to participate. However, there are few disappointments as deep as creating a book that doesn't sell. I know. I started there. I discovered how to do it wrong long before I figured out how to do it right. It took some diligent research and some hard knocks to finally get it right. This book is the starting point to endless possibilities that will actually bring results rather than disappointments.

There are a number of factors that go into a bestselling book on Amazon. Those factors come down to two important principles: discoverability and conversion. What I mean by these two are simply that the book has to have mechanisms that help it be "discovered" by the exact people who might buy it, and the second one means that it has to then appeal to them enough that they convert into paying customers and purchase the book.

I'm going to discuss the factors that create a book that is discoverable and that converts or sells. There are many of them, and I will touch on the most important ones, but I intend to show you how to easily discover the topics, niches, and titles that will have the best chances of making continual sales.

I am a firm believer in following working models, so I am going to show you how to find models that work, and show you examples of how to discover and mimic those models for your ultimate success.

I am a number one bestselling author. Below is a screen capture of one of my books during a time when it was a number one best seller for two Amazon categories.

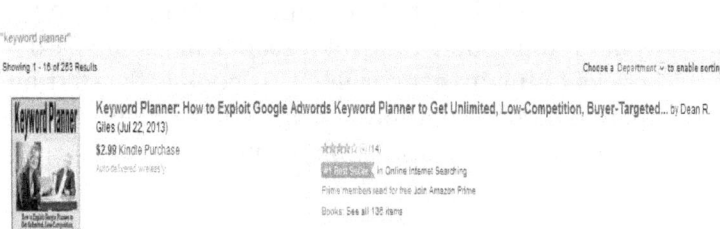

Figure 1 Amazon Best Seller

I have written books that sell five or more copies per day, and I have written books that may sell one copy every other month.

I was frustrated that my first books really didn't sell well in spite of all of the personal time and money that I put into promoting them. I decided to do some real research, and have since read more than one hundred books, eBooks, courses, articles, and posts related to writing, publishing, and marketing books and eBooks. The methods that I developed from that research have changed my perspective about writing, but most of all have changed my success rate.

It is my hope and desire to save you the pain and frustration that I went through and help you to make your first book, and every book thereafter, a good selling asset and an endeavor worth pursuing. Writing has been very fulfilling to me. I love solving people's problems, and enjoy receiving email and comments from people who I have helped along the way.

After reading this eBook, if you feel like you have benefitted from these pages at all, I hope that you would share what you have learned with others. Let them know that they can also profit from writing if they approach it in a simple, straight forward, and systematic way. I will show you how easy that can really be and actually how much fun it can be.

Start With the End in Mind

This is truly the most important part of writing a book. What do you want to accomplish with writing a book? If you are hoping to sell your books to make some extra cash, then what topic will you choose to write about? What problems will you help people to solve? How will people find your book? Does a book on that topic really have a chance of being discovered and purchased by lots of people?

Chris Anderson, in his book, *The Long Tail*, explained that there is a market for almost anything, but the number of participants in that market gets fewer and fewer as the purchasers move away from the central products at the "big head" and glide towards the more specific products down the marketing tail.

Without trying to explain his entire book, I just want to relate some statistics to the above paragraph. Let's say that the most popular books on a certain subject make up 50% or more of all of the sales of books on that subject. Those books make up the "big head," and the percentages of sales drop off significantly as we get further and further away from that cluster of the most popular books.

What an author needs to do is to write about a topic that is so closely related to those most popular books, that their books are not very far away on the graph from the popular ones. They will want to discover a gap in the offerings that are available, and be able to fill that gap in a way that really meets customer needs and wants. Doing it in a creative way that brings out your own unique style and voice will create the magic that will sell your book. What I want to do with this book is to teach you how to find those "niche" topics that have a chance at really doing well and help you integrate those ideas into your writing.

Kindle Niches

I intend to focus on niches for Kindle eBooks for a number of reasons: I have had success with Kindle eBooks, Amazon will help you market them when they appear to be selling well, and because the markets for eBooks are exploding right now. The methods that I teach, however, can be used for discovering niches that would be good as niche websites, membership sites, ezine articles, Youtube videos, Udemy courses, or pretty much anything that requires niche type writing.

What is a Niche?

A niche is a market segmentation that is suitable or appropriate for a specific endeavor. In this case, there are general subjects or topics that are large and made up of several subtopics. The subtopics could then be broken down into several niches. These niches could be thought of as even smaller subtopics that are very specific. I'm going to be showing you what niches look like, how to recognize good ones, and how to, kind of validate that they would do well as a Kindle eBook.

Niches From Bestsellers

Model success in all that you do.

Success breeds success, it is a true principle. People are judged by association, sometimes incorrectly, but often people tend to be like those that they associate with. You want your book to be successful by being associated with other successful books.

Signs of Success on Amazon

It may or may not seem obvious, but Amazon gives you lots of hints about what books are selling well that are associated with your interests, your buying habits, and your search habits. Amazon also has a number of lists that associate books. You really want your book associated with books that are selling well.

To find a niche, you need to deconstruct your search from the major topic to the subtopics and finally down to the very specific niches. There are so many ways to do this, and I will discuss many of those ways over the course of this book.

However, to set the stage for understanding how to get to the niches, I need you to select a major topic that you might have some interest in. It can be any topic. For this example, I am going to choose the topic of golf. I don't know this for a fact, but I believe that there are a lot of people who have an interest in golf, so I will pick that topic out of "thin air".

You need to find good topics to write about, but you can't spend a lot of time on researching the right topics, because you need to spend most of that time writing. This is how to do your research quickly. Get a paper and pencil out, or open a document where you are going to keep the ideas for niches as you run into them. I'm going to use a number of topics and niches as examples. You may not be interested in golf or any of the other subjects that I use as examples, but I want you to take time out to try these exercises with a subject that you are interested in, so simply have the tools ready so that you can write down niche ideas as you come across them.

Using the Kindle Store

The first thing that I am going to do is go to Amazon.com, and select the Kindle Store from the search bar. Then I am going to type golf in at the search bar, and then select "image", then finally click go.

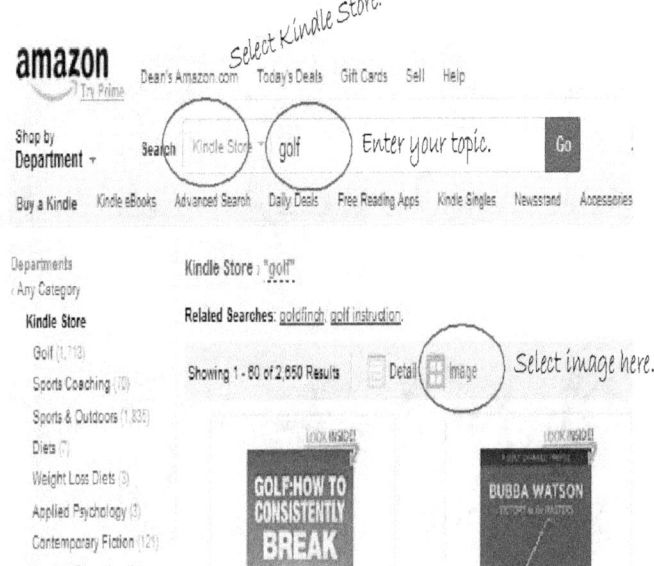

Figure 2 Amazon Search

A page of books about golf will be displayed as shown in the figure below.

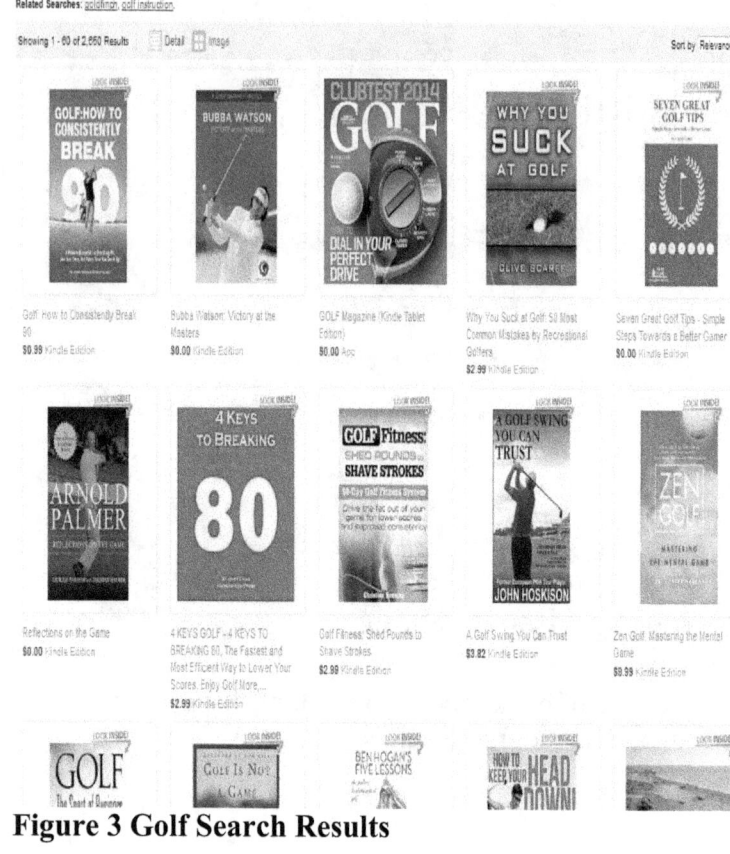

Figure 3 Golf Search Results

At the top of the screen you will see a message: "showing 1-60 of 2,650 results". This is definitely a broad topic that has a lot of interest. There could be many, many niches inside of this broad category.

It is important to note, however, that we haven't determined whether any of these books are selling. That can be determined by clicking on the individual titles. If you take the first of the books that are not on free promotion and click on it, you will see the following in the product details section.

Product Details

File Size: 2900 KB

Print Length: 55 pages

Publisher: IGD Publishing (August 30, 2013)

Sold by: Amazon Digital Services, Inc.

Language: English

ASIN: B00EWU8OES

Text-to-Speech: Enabled

X-Ray: Not Enabled

Lending: Enabled

Amazon Best Sellers Rank: #36,889 Paid in Kindle Store (See Top 100 Paid in Kindle Store)
    #16 in Kindle Store > Kindle eBooks > Nonfiction > Sports > Golf
    #37 in Books > Sports & Outdoors > Golf

Figure 4 Amazon Best Seller Rank

Near the bottom of the screen the Amazon Best Seller Rank: #36,889 is displayed. This number represents where the book is relative to all other books selling on Amazon. It states that as far as sales go, it is selling better than all of the millions of books on Amazon except for the 36,888 books that rank ahead of it. The ranks are recalculated often, and although they don't have a set conversion for how many copies of the book are being sold, the best seller rank can give you a rough idea of where the book stands. A best seller rank of 50,000 produces, on average, between 1 and 3 sales per day. Although the rank of 50,000 is somewhat arbitrary, it is one that I like to shoot for. I am looking for three or more eBooks that rank below 50,000 somewhere in the first 20 books listed. I am even more interested in a topic if it has one or two listed below the 20,000 rank.

This list is for the broad category, however, we will want to narrow down the scope of our intended book even further than this. There are some great hints as to what those narrowed subtopics might look like.

Related Searches

At the top of the screen of figure 3, the screen produced by searching for our golf topic, there are a couple of links to "related" searches. There are two links, but the "goldfinch" link doesn't really apply to our topic. The other one, "golf instruction", does, and should be one of the next searches that we try. The Golf Instruction search has fewer titles, but some of the titles sell even better than the general titles that we looked at previously.

Customers Who Bought This Also Bought

Right below the product description of each book is a section called "customers who bought this also bought". This section looks like the figure below:

Customers Who Bought This Item Also Bought

The Sweet Spot. Great Golf Starts Here. ...	4 KEYS GOLF - HOW TO BREAK 90 (An Easy ...	4 KEYS GOLF - 4 KEYS TO BREAKING 80, ...	A Golf Swing You Can Trust	Why You Suck at Golf: 50 Most Common Mistakes ...
Geoff Greig	Andy Chao	Andy Chao	John Hoskison	Clive Scarff
★★★★☆ (50)	★★★☆☆ (23)	★★★★☆ (26)	★★★★☆ (31)	★★★★☆ (48)
Kindle Edition	Kindle Edition	Kindle Edition	Kindle Edition	Kindle Edition
$4.99	$2.99	$2.99	$3.82	$2.99

Figure 5 Customers Who Bought This Item Also Bought

Here are some other books that might be better segmented into a subtopic. Whatever your topic of interest is, write down the titles of the books that come up that look interesting and are related to your topic.

Another source of bestselling book titles is BarnesAndNoble.com. Type in your topic name at the search bar on top. For this example I am going to use "be healthy" as my seed keyword or my broad topic.

Read the rest of the book here:
https://www.amazon.com/dp/B00IODSNVI

Other Books by This Author:

About Writing

How to Steal Like an Author:
http://www.amazon.com/dp/B00NVN99FK
Discover Book Ideas:
http://www.amazon.com/dp/B00IODSNVI
Write On
http://www.amazon.com/dp/B00O9LIBMK
How to Outline a book
https://www.amazon.com/dp/B077PP977T

Not About Writing

Dragons Restored
http://www.amazon.com/dp/B014N2E9CU
Life's Poetry
http://www.amazon.com/dp/B00UU0UQ2C
Poems of Love
https://www.amazon.com/dp/B079Z1GN5
M
The Snow Birthday
http://www.amazon.com/dp/B00BWAP6SS
Summer Time Fun
http://www.amazon.com/dp/B00DZVYG4
W
Keyword Planner
http://www.amazon.com/dp/B00E45ADKE

Connect with me

Email: dean@autstinsgift.com
Blog: http://austinsgift.com
Facebook:
https://www.facebook.com/WriteAStepByStepBoo
k

Stressed? Try an Adult coloring book

Get Your Free Gift!

Please register to download your free gift
at http://austinsgift.com/gift/ .

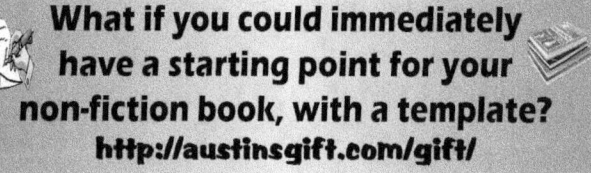

Appendix

Facebook Book Groups

https://www.facebook.com/groups/4262821374325
33/

https://www.facebook.com/groups/389343847782037/

https://www.facebook.com/groups/pageoneprofits/

https://www.facebook.com/groups/BooksLuvers/

https://www.facebook.com/groups/abrex/

https://www.facebook.com/groups/passionforbooks/

https://www.facebook.com/groups/childrenbookclub/

https://www.facebook.com/groups/Bookjunkiesfreebies/

https://www.facebook.com/groups/bookplace/

https://www.facebook.com/groups/freetoday/

https://www.facebook.com/groups/270558336379692/

https://www.facebook.com/groups/157960580960255/

https://www.facebook.com/groups/memberswritersgroup/

https://www.facebook.com/groups/469592073074586/

https://www.facebook.com/groups/KidBooksWithGoodValues/

https://www.facebook.com/groups/AmazonBookClubs/

https://www.facebook.com/groups/187547284642012/

https://www.facebook.com/groups/booknest/

https://www.facebook.com/groups/174224899314282/

https://www.facebook.com/groups/623206594363552/

https://www.facebook.com/groups/ebooksrock/

https://www.facebook.com/groups/kindlemojo/

https://www.facebook.com/groups/2204546223/

https://www.facebook.com/groups/204725947524/
https://www.facebook.com/groups/booksgoneviral/
https://www.facebook.com/groups/iluvbooks/
https://www.facebook.com/groups/2204565182/
https://www.facebook.com/groups/320356974732142/
https://www.facebook.com/groups/179494068820033/
https://www.facebook.com/groups/bookjunkiepromotions/
https://www.facebook.com/groups/436402966439126/
https://www.facebook.com/groups/freebkrus/
https://www.facebook.com/groups/boomdom/
https://www.facebook.com/groups/370900356880/
https://www.facebook.com/groups/kindlemarketingrevelations/
https://www.facebook.com/groups/ParaYourAbnormalAuthors/
https://www.facebook.com/groups/FreeTodayOnAmazon/
https://www.facebook.com/groups/ReviewersRoundup/
https://www.facebook.com/groups/9476163038/
https://www.facebook.com/groups/freeebooks/
https://www.facebook.com/groups/1402168653333862/

Places to Post Your Kindle Select Free Days

http://ereadernewstoday.com/ent-free-book-submissions/

http://www.fkbooksandtips.com/for-authors/free-kindle-book-submission-form/

http://digitalbooktoday.com/12-top-100-submit-your-free-book-to-be-included-on-this-list/

http://indiebookoftheday.com/authors/free-on-kindle-listing/

http://rastephensonauthor.blogspot.com/p/free-promotion-for-independent-authors.html

http://www.mybookandmycoffee.com/p/free-ebook-feature.html

http://freedigitalreads.com/author-submissions/

http://indieauthorbookreviews.wordpress.com/kindle-promo/

http://www.sevenbillionereaderbooks.com/free-kindle-book-submission/

http://www.pixelofink.com/sfkb/

http://bargainebookhunter.com/free-book-notification-form/

http://kindlenationdaily.com/kindle-nation-daily-free-and-bargain-book-listings/

http://www.freebooksifter.com/?c=7

http://www.dailyfreebooks.co.uk/promote-your-kindle-book.html

http://onehundredfreebooks.com/author-free-kindle-book-submission.html

http://www.ebookxp.net/submit.php

http://www.totallyfreestuff.com/submit.asp?m=0

http://www.icravefreebies.com/contact/
http://bargainebookhunter.com/feature-your-book/
http://addictedtoebooks.com/free#comment-3747
http://ebookshabit.com/for-authors/
http://www.theereadercafe.com/p/authors.html
http://www.freebookdude.com/p/list-your-free-book.html
http://www.frugal-freebies.com/p/submit-freebie.html

Facebook Pages to List Free Books On

These are quick and easy, just go to the pages on your free day, and put a link to your Kindle eBook in the post. They appear immediately.

https://www.facebook.com/Freebies4Mom
https://www.facebook.com/bookskindle
https://www.facebook.com/FreeBookFeed
https://www.facebook.com/KindleUtopia
https://www.facebook.com/pages/Free-Daily-eBooks/277545182364423
https://www.facebook.com/FreeEbooksDownloads
https://www.facebook.com/eReaderLove
https://www.facebook.com/KindleFreebies
https://www.facebook.com/ePublish.a.Book
https://www.facebook.com/pages/Free-Kindle-Books-Updated-Daily/155923931093850

Resources / Bibliography

Giles, Dean, *Keyword Planner: How to Exploit Google Adwords Keyword Planner to Get Unlimited, Buyer-Targeted, Long-Tail Key*words, http://www.amazon.com/Keyword-Planner-Low-Competition-Buyer-Targeted-Instruction-ebook/dp/B00E45ADKE/

Aaron, Rachel, *2,000 to 10,000: Writing Faster, Writing Better, Writing More Of What You Love*, http://www.amazon.com/2k-10k-Writing-Faster-Better-ebook/dp/B009NKXAWS/

Allen, Christopher David, *How to Publish a #1 Best Seller On Kindle – No Cost Publishing and Marketing Secrets of a Bestselling Author – How to Book and Guide for Smart Dummies*, http://www.amazon.com/HOW-PUBLISH-BEST-SELLER-KINDLE-ebook/dp/B0089TESCU/

Becker, Dennis, *One Problem Product Creation*, http://incomenow.org/one-problem-ebook

Covey, Steven R., *7 Habits of Highly Effective People: Powerful Lessons in Personal Change*, http://www.amazon.com/Habits-Highly-Effective-People-Anniversary-ebook/dp/B00GOZV3TM/

Drum, Deb and Harrop, Amy, *Description Detective 2*, http://incomenow.org/description-detective2

Eagle, Dennis and Villegas, Oliver, *7 Secret Steps to Best Selling Author*, http://www.amazon.com/Secret-Steps-Bestselling-Author-Revealed-ebook/dp/B00EA1XGJW/

Kindle Direct Publishing, *Building Your Book for Kindle*, http://www.amazon.com/Building-Your-Kindle-Direct-Publishing-ebook/dp/B007URVZJ6/

Locke, John, *How I Sold 1 Million eBooks in 5 Months*, http://www.amazon.com/How-Sold-Million-eBooks-Months-ebook/dp/B0056BMK6K/

Redwine, Kate, *Crush It With Kindle Publishing The Entrepreneur's Guide for Self Publishing Books on Kindle, and Promoting Your Book to #1 Bestseller Status*, http://www.amazon.com/Publishing-Entrepreneurs-Building-Promoting-Bestseller-ebook/dp/B00DH8STT6/

Rofe, Rachel, KInstant Formatter, http://incomenow.org/KinstantFormatter

Kleon, Austin, *Steal Like an Artist: 10 Things No One Told You About Creativity*, http://www.amazon.com/Steal-Like-Artist-Things-Creative-ebook/dp/B0074QGGK6/

LJS Quote 2 Motivate, *Quotes For Writers: Inspiration, Advice, Humor, and Motivational Stories From Famous Authors*, http://www.amazon.com/Quotes-Writers-Inspiration-Motivational-Stories-ebook/dp/B00HFA4V9O/

Plat, Sean and Truant, Johnny B., *Write. Publish. Repeat.*, http://www.amazon.com/Publish-Repeat-No-Luck-Required-Self-Publishing-Success-ebook/dp/B00H26IFJS/

Scott, Steve, *How to Discover Bestselling eBook Ideas – The Bulletproof Strategy*, http://www.amazon.com/Discover-Best-Selling-Nonfiction-eBook-Ideas-ebook/dp/B009D6JL20/

Tardif, Cheryl Kaye, *How I Made $42,000 In One Month Selling My Kindle eBooks*, http://www.amazon.com/Made-Month-Selling-Kindle-eBooks-ebook/dp/B0080USSYW/

Turner, Laina, *All I Know About eBook Marketing*, http://www.amazon.com/All-Know-About-e-Book-Marketing-ebook/dp/B009VO9YGW/

Vulich, Nick, *Freeking Idiots Guide to Writing a Kindle Bestseller Tips and Tricks to Make Your Book a Bestseller in Its Category*, http://www.amazon.com/Freaking-Writing-Bestseller-bestseller-category-ebook/dp/B00B1Z7YFM/

Williams, Glyn, *Bestseller Tactics: Advanced Self Publishing Techniques to Help You Sell More Books On Amazon and Make More Money. Advanced Author Marketing.* http://www.amazon.com/Bestseller-Tactics-publishing-techniques-Marketing-ebook/dp/B00GHTL5O8/